When Seasons Change

Linda Scott

Book Description

To everything, there is a season and seasons do change. In this book, you will receive encouragement to go through the process and transition associated with your season. The Word of God helps you navigate your season and give you confidence, trust, and assurance that no matter the crushing of the season, God will not abandon you. This book ignites and stirs up strength for the believer in trusting the process of their season, for it is God who changes times and seasons. Embrace your process. Embrace your season. Don't avoid it, for seasons do change.

Copyright © 2019 Linda Scott. All rights reserved. Published 2019.

PurposeHouse Publishing, Columbia, Maryland

ISBN: 978-0-9963647-2-0

No part of this publication may be reproduced or distributed in any form or by any means, or stored in a database or retrieval system, without the prior written permission of the publisher. Email requests for permission to ministeringpurpose@gmail.com.

Unless otherwise indicated, all scriptural quotations are from the King James Version of the Bible, which is in the public domain.

Scripture from the American Standard Version (ASV), public domain

Scripture from Amplified Bible (AMP, Copyright © 1987 by the Lockman Foundation. (www.Lockman.org))

American Bible Classic Edition (AMPC, Copyright © by the Lockman Foundation. (www.Lockman.org))

Scripture from the Contemporary English Version (CEV), Copyright © 1995 by American Bible Society

Complete Jewish Bible (CJB), Copyright © 1998 by David H. Stern.

English Standard Version (ESV), Copyright © 2001 by Crossway, a publishing ministry of Good News Publishers.

Scripture from the Living Bible (TLB), copyright © 1971 by Tyndale House Foundation, Used by permission of Tyndale

House Publishers Inc., Carol Stream, Illinois 60188. All rights reserved.

Scripture from the Message Bible (MSG), Copyright © 1993, 1994, 1995, 1996, 2000, 2001, 2002 by Eugene H. Peterson, All rights reserved

Scripture from the New International Version (NIV), Copyright © 1973, 1978, 1984 by Biblica.

Scripture from New King James Version (NKJV), Copyright © 1982 by Thomas Nelson, Inc., All rights reserved.

Scripture from the New Life Version (NLV), Copyright © 1969 by Christian Literature International.

Scripture from the New Living Translation (NLT), Copyright © 1996, 2004 by Tyndale Charitable Trust.

Scripture from the Wycliffe Bible (WYC), copyright © 2001 by Terence P. Noble.

Dedication

I dedicate this book to my mom, Frances Toogood. You are such a tenacious, vibrant woman of great strength.

Contents

Chapter 1	To Everything, There is a Season	13
Chapter 2	Seasons	15
Chapter 3	The Encounter	17
Chapter 4	The Assignment	21
Chapter 5	The Process	25
Chapter 6	Between Seasons	33
Chapter 7	The Promise	39

Introduction

We are living in a time where comfortability is the order of the day. As long as we consider ourselves safe, we label it as happiness. Imagine that it is a beautiful spring day. The sun is shining, the sky is clear, and the trees have blossomed with different yet beautiful roses and flowers. Everyone is making plans to enjoy the weather; and then, suddenly—here comes a storm to rain on your parade. What happened? Life happened. Seasons changed.

Chapter 1
To Everything, There is a Season

If it is winter, we say that it is too cold; if it is summer, we say it's too hot; and, if it is fall, we say the leaves falling from the trees are a nuisance. If it is spring, we complain about the rain. No matter what season you may be encountering, seasons do change. On this journey, we will encounter some hills and some valleys; and yet also have some mountaintop experiences.
It is necessary to make the proper adjustments to the climate changes in our lives to be sustained in a season that seems lifeless. When enduring seasons of trials, challenges, hardships, and setbacks, there is one thing that you must hold on to--the assurance in knowing that every season has an expiration date.

Seasons do change.

As a child growing up in a world so big and seemingly so

bright, I had the audacity to dream big. I dared to utilize an imagination of untainted thoughts, possessing a boldness, conveying the strength of a lion, and the pure innocence of a dove.

In a world of limitless possibilities, I never imagined that my greatest cheerleaders, my mom, and my dad, would not always be by my side. Seasons change.

Chapter 2
Seasons

There was a time I thought that seasons only pertained to the weather. After becoming a student of the Word of God, I came to understand that Seasons are periods of time. They are periods that we find ourselves encountering life-matters: from times of excitement to moments of pleasure, to frustration and despair. There are even times of grasping for breath while, day to day, we strive to endure chaos.

In Ecclesiastes 3:1-8 (New International Version), we find comfort and assurance in knowing that there is a time for everything.

> There is a time for everything, and a season for every activity under the heavens:　a time to be born and a time to die, a time to plant and a time to uproot,　a time to kill and a time to heal, a time to tear down and a time to build, a time to weep and a time to laugh, a time to mourn and a time to dance, a time to scatter stones and a

time to gather them, a time to embrace and a time to refrain from embracing, a time to search and a time to give up, a time to keep and a time to throw away, a time to tear and a time to mend, a time to be silent and a time to speak, a time to love and a time to hate, a time for war and a time for peace.

These scriptures confirm that we will go through different seasons in our lives.

Sometimes, life can become very consuming and frustrating when we neglect to deal with the hurt, unresolved issues, and unmet needs in our lives. I remember balling up in the fetal position every time I became swallowed up by disappointment. I remember having a temper tantrum when things did not go as I planned. Then, one day I had an encounter with God!

Chapter 3
The Encounter

We are sent here as God's chosen ambassadors in the earth to demonstrate, legislate, and dominate the work of the kingdom of God. Somehow, between coming from one dimension into the earth (entering into another dimension), we became so distracted by life processes that it now takes a ***suddenly*** in our lives to shake us and wake us. We need an awakening so that there can be a coming together and an oneness with the one who has sent us to this place called earth. That shaking, that pressing, that shifting has many faces, shapes, and forms, such as pain, trauma, grief, rejection, abandonment, loneliness, low self-worth, low self-esteem, depression, infirmity/sickness, loss, and the list goes on and on and on.

While at my salon doing hair, I heard this soft voice. It began to overpower my thoughts, extending an invitation for me to come, a call for me to come out. Hurrying along as fast as I could to finish my client's hair; finally, I finished. I could not escort her out of the salon door soon enough before pulling the curtains and dropping on my knees. With both hands covering my ears, as if I could silence him, the overpowering voice continued to say, "How long will you run. I have a plan for your life." Tears began to flood my face. I was balled up in the fetal position saying who or what is this; and the voice replied, "It's me, Jesus. And I have a plan for your life." I yelled, "Stop talking to me. Go away," because the voice was so calm yet overpowering. The Lord knew that I had already planned to go and shoot the individual that I had been in a relationship with for seven years. The pain, agony, hurt, betrayal, abuse, fighting, and drama had me at a breaking point that I could not verbalize. No one around me knew I was drowning, dying on the inside. It was that day I conversed with Jesus saying, "Go away," that Jesus continued to assure me that there was a plan for my life—that I knew nothing about.

After hours into this encounter, the Lord told me to arise. He led me to the front door to gaze out of the window and said, "Look." When I looked, the Lord opened my eyes in an open vision, and I saw Martin Luther King preaching to thousands. A second time, the Lord said, "Look." When I looked again, I saw myself doing the same thing. I remember seeing chains, shackles, and yokes breaking off of people and this freaked me out. I fell to the floor weeping under the power of God.

Later, when I came to myself, the Lord instructed me to walk away from that relationship, lifestyle, and unhealthy, vicious cycle that I had been living in for seven years. The Lord said, "Walk away. It will be ok." And I was honest with the Lord saying, "I don't know you to trust you." And that day, the Lord said, "Let me prove to you who I am." From that day, the Lord freed me and broke the bars and the irons that held me captive, destroying the yoke of homosexuality, perversion, promiscuous bondages, and exotic entertainment off of my life. From that time until now, God has proven to be faithful and consistent. In spite of what we have seen in our lives, every season we have encountered has an assignment. Seasons change.

Before I became accustomed to walking in an intimate relationship with the Lord, I was not sensitive to the whispers of his voice. And as a result, I used to find myself easily frustrated about my journey. Thank God for the plan! Jeremiah 29:11 says, I know the thoughts that I have towards you.

Chapter 4
The Assignment

Whenever you receive an assignment, you have to look closely at the context that the instructor has given.

Many times, people go out of their way to try to make their life line up with their goals, their plans, and their *Roberts Rules of Order* of how they believe things should happen or unfold. But as we all know, everything has a season. In all the chaos, in the midst of all we have gone through, we are still in our right mind. After we have endured a lot of blows, after we have suffered lots of hits, after we have experienced levels of betrayal, and broken relationships, we must be reminded that we still have an assignment!

In Isaiah 61:1, we see that the Lord has anointed us for an assignment. The Prophet declares that the anointing of God has come upon him for an assignment.

The Lord has placed something in you. The Lord has placed an anointing upon your life for you to fulfill something in the earth. There has been something tailor-made and prescribed for every one of us. We have come into the earth with an assignment, and that assignment is to fulfill heaven's mandate.

Whenever you receive an assignment, you have to look closely at the context in which your instructor has prescribed to understand how to set your standards, and how to set yourself in the right posture and position to fulfill the mandate of your instructor. For you to be able to satisfy the instructor's request, or to make sure you properly align yourself with the mandate of the instructor, you have to make sure you understand the rules of engagement.

The Prophet declares that the Spirit of the Lord has come upon him. We have to understand that the Spirit of the Lord does not just walk around to do nothing, the Spirit of the Lord comes upon us for an assignment, to fulfill a mandate so that we can fulfill a specific assignment. The Bible declares that we are created, formed, and made to fulfill an assignment. That means we are created to bring God glory.

Often, we start this journey but find ourselves getting off of the original course simply because we started thinking that it was about us and what we wanted, needed, and desired. We don't realize that if it's all about us and what we want, if it's all about what we need, and what we desire; then, how is it that God can get the glory? How, then, are we able to fulfill the assignment? Whenever the Lord gives us an assignment, the Spirit of the Lord comes upon us to assist us in fulfilling that assignment.

We have to understand the Trinity, their roles, and how they operate. We understand that God, being the Father, and the Holy Spirit's assignment, being our teacher, is to lead and guide us into all truth. When the Prophet Isaiah declares, in Isaiah 61, that the Spirit of the Lord has come upon him, it means he has anointed him. He has authorized Isaiah. He has empowered him. He has strengthened him to fulfill the mandate and to make sure that, that mandate is fulfilled.

God does the same thing for you and me. His Spirit comes upon you and me. The Lord takes your spirit and conforms you. He takes your spirit and transforms you. He takes your spirit and renovates it so that it is no longer you that lives; but it is Christ that lives in you. Then he allows his Spirit to come upon you to fulfill the mandate. The first thing the Spirit of the Lord did when he came upon the Prophet was authorization and second, validation to fulfill the mandate.

I had not raised my hand to sign up for this journey, but the Spirit of the Lord took me through some processes to get me ready. I had to go down some challenging roads to get ready, and just like you, your process also has an assignment to get you ready for your Season. For your Season is about to change.

Chapter 5
The Process

What is process? Process is a series of particular steps taken in order to achieve a particular end. During the process, we go through many different stages. These stages never seem to be comfortable; but will later become favorable. In fact, whenever you are in the process stage, it is important to remember that it is just that—process not promise. Let's look at the incubator process.

The Incubator Process

An incubator is an enclosed apparatus, providing a controlled environment for the care and protection of premature or unusually small babies. This is a sensitive part of the process because it is here that you will find God introducing himself to his people.

God is trying to get your attention.
Before God does anything, he always

gives you the forecast through the Word or through his Prophet/servants.

Whenever God is getting ready to dialog with you, you will find that he does this by first introducing himself either through his Word or through his servants.

Psalms 100:3 declares, No ye that the Lord is God it is he that made us and not we ourselves, we are his people and the sheep of his Pasture. So God is letting us know that we did not make ourselves. We belong to him. And because we belong to him, he should be able to speak to us and we obey him because we belong to him! Just the same, as parents we expect our children to obey us because they belong to us. The Bible declares that we belong to God. Isaiah 43:1 declares, but now thus saith the LORD that created thee, O Jacob, and he that formed thee, O Israel, Fear not: for I have redeemed thee, I have called thee by thy name; thou art mine. This chapter opens up letting you know, I am the Lord that created thee. So God is letting you know, I am getting ready to speak to you. I am getting ready to have a dialog with you. I am getting ready to speak to you about a contract, about an agreement. But before I speak to you, I need to make sure you understand four things:

1. I have created you.
2. I have formed you.
3. I have redeemed you.
4. I have called you.

Before God does anything, his pattern shows us he starts by

introducing himself and reintroducing himself to show us who he is. Remember Isaiah 43:1 says, But now thus saith the LORD that created thee, O Jacob, and he that formed thee, O Israel, Fear not: for I have redeemed thee, I have called thee by thy name; thou art mine. Who is God with? He is with those that he created, formed, redeemed, and has called. Something happens when the Lord begins to speak. (Genesis 1:3) When God begins to speak something is created: When God speaks something is formed. When God opens his mouth something is manifested. When God speaks something happens.

In Isaiah 43, God starts off letting us know I created you, I formed you, I redeemed you, and I have called you by name. Every time God opens his mouth, something manifests. According to Genesis 1:27, God created us in his image and in his likeness. Whatever God desired to see, he spoke it and he named it. In Genesis 2:18, God is speaking what he wants to manifest. Genesis 2:19 says, and out of the ground the Lord God formed every living creature of the field and every bird of the air and brought them unto Adam to see what he would call them and what so ever Adam called them that was the name there of. Don't you see, when God speaks there is a creation. When God speaks, he forms things. When God speaks, there is a manifestation. God speaks things into existence; but wait, don't get stuck there. Genesis 1:27 says, so God created man in his own image, in the image and likeness of God, he created them.

God has given you the same power he has. He shows us by way of Isaiah 43, I am the Lord God of Jacob. He shows us here that he is reintroducing himself to us personally. God has created us for his glory. Isaiah 43 says, I have created you, I have called you, and I have formed you, Fear not. God opens his mouth to create what he wants to see and because he has created you in his image, he has declared that you shall do even greater works. The chapter talks about God redeeming his people. It opens with God reintroducing himself saying, I am the God that created you. I am the God that formed you. Fear not. I have already redeemed you. Fear not. I have already called you by your name. Specifically, God tells us to fear not. Before we go deeper into the chapter, we do not even know yet what he is telling us not to fear.

But, he is letting us know that if we go through the waters or through the fire, he is going to be right there. Fear not. God says, before I show you what is ahead I need to make sure you understand that I am introducing myself to these people. I am introducing myself to the people that I created, the people that I formed, the people that I called by name. These are the people that the Lord is talking to in Isaiah 43:5. The Lord tells us, fear not. I am with thee. I am with those that I have created, formed, redeemed, and called.

God has a way of making sure you understand that you are his people. When God opens his mouth, everything starts shifting. Stuff starts forming. There is a shaking and a coming together. God calls us specifically by our name. He does not want us to get confused and assume he is just talking to anybody. He wants to make sure we are clear that he is speaking specifically to us. Fear not, for I have called you by your name. Fear not, when thou pass through the waters I will be with you, and through the rivers they will not overwhelm you. When thou walk through the fire, you will not be burned. No matter where you are in your process, your creator said "Fear not." Your redeemer said, "Fear not." The one that created you says, "Fear not." Your protector said, "Far not." Although weeping may endure for a night, fear not. For I am with you, says the lord. Fear not, because I have called you by name.

God wants to make sure you understand the contract. He wants to make sure you understand the rules of engagement. He wants to make sure that no matter what part of the process you are in, or what you are up against, he says fear not. He tells us from the beginning that I am your redeemer, the one that created you. I have called you by name. Fear not.

Isaiah 43:7 says, even everyone that is called by my name, I have formed him, and I have created him for my glory. A lot of times, we want to make it look like it's about us and start binding the devil. But in verse 8, it says bring forth the blind people that has eyes and the deaf people that has ears because today the Lord is opening up your eyes. Today the scales are falling off your eyes and today your ears are being unclogged.

Fear not. Where you are and what you are in has been orchestrated by the Father. The Lord has allowed you to go through the very thing that you are in for his glory. This is not about you. In Isaiah 43:7, the Bible declares, fear not because I have created you for my glory. Every one that has been called by my name has been created for my glory.

We are binding up the works of the devil and telling him this and that when God has already told us fear not. That thing that you are dealing with has been designed to bring God glory. Is there anyone reading this book on today that will allow God to take you through a process so that he can get glory?, Is there anyone reading this book on today that says, my eyes are being opened so that I can truly say, "God I see it for myself, that you have formed me, you have created me, you have redeemed me, you have called me by name? You have already saved me before you took me through it, you have already saved me before you called me by my name?" The Lord says, fear not. Where you are is not unto your death. You are in the right position to bring me glory.

Like our friends (the children of Israel), we find ourselves having been a selfish people. Like they did in Exodus, we find ourselves jumping and shouting as long as things are happening the way we want. But as soon as it reverses and goes opposite of what we wanted, we return back to an old mindset of murmuring and complaining. But you have to understand, God is trying to prove you. He is trying to posture you to be like the Hebrew boys who believed come what may, our God can deliver us and if he doesn't—he is still God. Fear not. We see by way of the book of Genesis, that every time God opens his mouth to speak, something shows up. Every time God opens his mouth to declare such a thing, something shows up. In Genesis 1, God did an observation. He looked out over the face of the deep and there was nothing. And because there was nothing,

God decided to open his mouth. There is power when God opens his mouth. And let me remind you that you are created in the image and the likeness of God. So that means when you stop complaining and learn how to open your mouth, something will happen. Something moves, shakes, and happens when God begins to speak.

The Lord wants to make sure this contract, this agreement, these rules of engagements are illuminated so that his people can understand it properly. He wants you to understand his Word properly. He wants to make sure you understand your process properly. You want God to bring you out, but in order for him to bring you out, he has to first take you in. Therefore, no matter what part of the process you are in, God has given us a command to fear not. You are not going to declare his Word out of fear, doubt, uncertainty, or unbelief. There will not be any doubt in your mind or in your heart.

The reason why God has allowed you to go through this kind of process is so you can bring him glory. Stop crying about coming out of the process because you don't want to go through anything at all!   Let me ask you a question, if God don't allow you to go through it how can he get glory? If God don't put you in a situation, how can he bring you out of a situation? The Bible declares we are created for God to get glory. No matter what part of the process you may be in: persecution, isolation, humiliation, confusion, transitioning, longsuffering, or severe crushing, you will find that it is helpful to use the Word of God to help navigate you through your process. And remember, seasons change!

Thy word is a lamp unto my feet and a light unto my path. – Psalm 119:105

Chapter 6
Between Seasons

Sometimes, seasons are discouraging. They are especially discouraging when you are in transition and caught between three places: processing, transitioning, and promise. While all of these places are of great importance, each holds a different weight. In Daniel Chapter 2, the Bible makes it clear that it is God who changes times and seasons.

Moses was given the assignment to be the "designated driver" for Israel. He was chosen to lead the children of Israel out of bondage. In Exodus 6:1-7, the Lord promised to bring the children of Israel out of captivity. The prophet Jeremiah declared that they would go into captivity for a season, for a while, and then God would bring them out. As the stage is set, we see the Lord positioning them for their departure--just like many of us today. We heard a word from God. We heard the Lord say that he was going to bring us out; but when it appeared as if we were out of time, we panicked.

We torment ourselves with anxiety because it does not seem like the Lord is going to deliver in the time frame of our expected need. The Lord says I am going to bring my people out. I appeared to Abraham, Isaac, and Jacob as God Almighty. I did not make myself known to them in great acts or miracles; meaning, the way I did it for them may not be the same way I do it for you. Verses 6-7 state, I will take you to me for a people, and I will be to you a God, who brings you out from under the burdens of the Egyptians. The process you have to go through will help you personally know that he is the Lord God Almighty.

Verse 8 says, I the Lord am bringing you into this place that I have chosen for you, this is a place that the Lord has chosen for us. God is taking us into this place because of the covenant connection. Because we are connected to Abraham, Isaac, and Jacob. Be careful who you are connecting to in this season. This is not a place that we have chosen for ourselves, but this is the place God has chosen for us. Because of his promise, God's Word cannot return back to him void.

For God to take us to the place that he promised, there are some processes that God will take us through so that it can come full circle, so that everything will come into divine alignment. God has promised to bring you out, and although we have shifted into another chapter, there still have to be other situations that show up for God to bring us out. Each time we see God give Moses instructions to tell Pharaoh let my people go, there has to be a cause. Meaning, for Pharaoh to let God's people go, there has to be a situation of enslavement, entanglement, bondage, or entrapment orchestrated by the Father so that he can bring you out with an outstretched hand.

There is a situation that no one else can fix but God. You are in the next chapter of your life. Now it is time to focus and organize a strategy. Life is still going to happen, and it does not mean that the weapons will prosper, but they will be formed. God has to bring you to a place of deliverance. How can he bring you to a place of deliverance if you are not in a place for him to deliver you from?

In this season of your life, prepare to be blessed because of a divine connection. God said I will give it to you for a heritage. Moses received instructions for the very people he had to lead and walk with through the process. He comes giving them the instruction of "thus says the Lord," and the Bible declares that they did not want to listen to Moses.

In verse 9, Moses told the people "thus says the Lord," but they refused to listen to Moses because of their impatience, anguish of spirit, and cruel bondage. Anguish can be emotional, physical, or spiritual. Anguish is sometimes the cause of suicide or homicide. People who experience psychological distress like anguish can have a higher risk of premature death.

So, when God uses a vessel to give you instructions to navigate through the land mine, you have to obey. You cannot be one that is impatient with the process. God has a strategic way and a strategic time to bring you out.

In verse 13, the Lord instructs Moses to go tell Pharaoh, "let my people go." Moses is like, this looks crazy. The people I am with will not even listen to me. How in the world will the enemy believe what I am saying and me and my own people are not even together? How is the enemy going to listen to what you are saying when you are divided?

How is the devil going to back up off of you when you do not stand for anything? You will not stand on the Word nor listen to the man or woman of God. You don't want anyone to tell you anything and you do not want anyone to give you instructions. You want to do it your way.

There is division in the camp of the ones to which Moses is called to give the Word. Moses is assigned to speak for murmuring, complaining people. They are in anguish and emotional and mad about their bondage. They are mad about their process. And out of all the people, God would choose Moses.

Imagine Moses over there frustrated because he cannot even get his speech together. He is frustrated about his speech, the people rejecting the Word, and trying to deliver the Word--then, they have a nerve not to listen. On top of that, God, you want me to go and declare this Word to the enemy (Pharaoh). The people that are with Moses won't listen. Pharaoh won't listen, and yet God tells Moses to get ready to be their escort.

It is normal to feel challenged when you have been in something for so long that seems like it will always be your reality. But in this place, when God tells you that he is going to bring you out, you have to make a decision to stand flat footed and unmovable. Do not allow the enemy to paralyze you with his tactics. Remember to walk by faith and not by sight. God has a strategic plan for your divine escape.

God tells Moses I have given you my command and instruction to carry it out. Behold, I make you like God to Pharaoh to declare my Word, my will, and my purpose. I make you like God to Pharaoh, means your authority is over the thing that looked like it was over you. Nothing but the purpose and the plan of God will stand.

> But Pharaoh shall not hearken unto you, that I may lay my hand upon Egypt, and bring forth mine armies, and my people the children of Israel, out of the land of Egypt by great judgments. And the Egyptians shall know that I am the Lord, when I stretch forth mine hand upon Egypt, and bring out the children of Israel from among them. (Exodus 7:4-5, KJV)

The only way your enemy will know your God is the processes you had to endure and what God brought you out of. People are watching you while you go through your process. The Bible declares, be ye transformed by the renewing of your mind. We must stay equipped and fully loaded with the Word of God at all times. When people see us, they should see the characteristics of Christ.

The enemy gets the opportunity to read the resume of our God by God allowing his people to go into captivity for the season. God moves when all of our resources are maxed out and time has elapsed. The Lord says, there are times that I have to intensify matters for my people to get an understanding of what I am saying. Although God hardened Pharaoh's heart while they were in bondage, God was also teaching his people that I the Lord am really who I say that I am.

Even until this very day, God demonstrates his capabilities through our process. We say with our mouth what we really do not demonstrate with our lifestyle. God continued to send Moses back and forth with a word for Pharaoh because all along, God was building something in Moses. Moses had on the job training, and if the truth be told, you too are in training while you are going through your process. But the Lord has assigned me to tell you that your wilderness experience is coming to an end. Get ready for your departure because your season is about to change.

God has positioned you for departure. Your season is changing. Even bringing them out of Egypt was a process. The process is necessary to help detox us from old paradigms. Seasons do change.

Chapter 7
The Promise

The promise shall stand. You are coming out of that thing that had you trapped. You are coming out of that thing that had you entangled. You are coming out of that place of captivity. It is set for an appointed time.

Every time we are given an instruction and we don't obey, it takes us through another set of processes. In order for God to bring us out, he has to take us in.

Get ready to shift into the promise of Isaiah 61:6-9 (Amplified Bible, Classic Edition) which says:

> [7] Instead of your [former] shame you shall have a twofold recompense; instead of dishonor *and* reproach [your people] shall rejoice in their portion. Therefore in their land they shall possess double [what they had forfeited]; everlasting joy shall be theirs. [8] For I the Lord love justice; I hate robbery *and* wrong with violence *or* a burnt offering. And I will faithfully give them their

recompense in truth, and I will make an everlasting covenant *or* league with them. ⁹ And their offspring shall be known among the nations and their descendants among the peoples. All who see them [in their prosperity] will recognize *and* acknowledge that they are the people whom the Lord has blessed.

God has a way to remind us of our future outcome, "People will speak of you as the ministers of God." In order for that to happen, there must be evidence that you belong to God. They will be able to look at you and know, without a doubt, that you have been called, you have been anointed, and validated, and you have been qualified by God. God has placed his anointing upon you so that when people see you there is evidence and it is obvious. There will be no mix up. In this day and time, that is extremely important because the Bible declares that there is a form of godliness that denies the power thereof. God is saying that the world is going to look upon you and there is going to be a distinct description and knowing that this is the man/woman of God that walks with the Spirit of the living God. There will not be an imposter or a misunderstanding when it comes to you because there will be evidence.

You shall be called the Priest of the Lord. People will speak of you as the ministers of God because there is going to be evidence present—not past tense but now! You shall eat the wealth of the nations and glory. Instead of your former shame, you shall have twofold recompense.

Recompense means to make amends to someone for loss, harm,

or suffering, to make amend to repay, to compensate, to give restitution, to reward and compensate for loss of harm suffered from efforts made. Isaiah 61:7 says, instead of your pass seasons of hardships and your former shame, you shall have twofold recompense, instead of dishonor and reproach your people shall rejoice in their portion therefore in their land they shall receive double. That means it's time for you to come out of your wilderness experience; it's time for you to come out of the desert; it's time for you time come out of your dry place; it's time for you to come out of the place of confusion; it's time for you to come out of the place of insufficiency; and, it's time for you to come out of the place of lack.

It's time for you to come out of the place unproductivity because it's time for you to step over into your land. Instead of your former shame, you shall have twofold recompense. Instead of dishonor and reproach, your people shall rejoice in their portion. Therefore, in their land, they shall possess double. You are not even going into your land with a little bit, trying to penny pinch thinking just in case something goes wrong or this is too good to be true. The Bible declares, therefore in their land they shall possess double of what they have forfeited. They will have everlasting joy. For I, the Lord, love justice, I hate robbery or violence, and wrong or burnt offering. And I will faithfully give them their recompense.

God says in this hour, it's time for justice. Your enemy is being dealt with right now because of the traps, plots, and lies that he has used to set up the people of God on a technicality. The enemy does a few things: he comes to kill, steal, and destroy.

The enemy has been getting the people of God on a technicality but God said that if you hold your peace and let the Lord fight your battle victory shall be yours. The thief comes to kill, steal, and destroy and, here we see in Isaiah 61:8, God says for I love justice. I hate robbery. I hate violence, but I will faithfully give my people recompense in truth. When God speaks a word and he says, it shall be, then it shall be.

In the beginning, God looked out over the face of the deep and said, let there be and it was so. He said, let there be light and it was light, it shall be this and it was so. And today, the Spirit of the Lord says it's time for you to push. It's time for you to deliver. It's time for you to shift gears. It's time for you to enter into the promise! There shall be no more delays. It's time for you to push and break out of that holding pattern. It's time for you to come into your destined place. In case you are wondering where my destined place is, the Bible declares in Isaiah 61:8, I will faithfully give them their recompense in truth and I will make an everlasting covenant and league with them. I am making an everlasting covenant that you shall be called the priest of the Lord, people will speak of you as ministers of God you shall eat the wealth of the nations and glory. Why? Because I have made an everlasting covenant with you.

God says my word is my truth and my word is *your* truth. Therefore, you shall no longer believe the lies of the enemy, you shall no longer settle for less than what God has called you to be, which is *the head*. God has called you to be his chosen generation, his royal priesthood. You shall eat the wealth of the nations and the glory that once was of your captors shall be yours.

Isaiah 61:9 says, their offspring shall be known among the nations and their descendants among the peoples. All who see them in their prosperity will recognize and acknowledge that they are the people whom the Lord has blessed. When the Lord blesses you, he blesses you no matter whose path you come across: those who thought that you were not going to make it, those that could have helped you so you could make it, and those who laid plots, traps, and landmines hoping that you were not going to survive it.

In Psalm 23:4, the Bible declares, he prepares a table before me in the presence of mine enemies. The party could not get started until David arrived. All who see them in their prosperity will recognize that they are the people whom the Lord has blessed! Isaiah 61:10 says, I will greatly rejoice in the Lord my soul will exult in my God. For he has clothed me with garments of salvation. He has covered me with the robe of righteousness. There have been times in all of our lives that we were unconscious to doing what was right. And there were times in our lives, no matter how hard we tried, it seemed as if we were colliding with a brick wall and coming up to a dead end. But thank God, for he has clothed me in garments of salvation and he has covered me with the robe of righteousness as a bridegroom decks himself with a garland and as a bride adorns herself with her jewels.

The spirit of the Lord says there is getting ready to be a divine release! Isaiah 61:11 says, for as surely as the earth brings forth her shoots and as a garden causes what was sown in it to spring forth. So {surely} the Lord God will cause rightness and justice and praise to spring forth before all the nations {through the self- fulfilling power of his word. What God is doing in your life will not be revoked. There is getting ready to be a divine release.

What God is doing cannot and will not be revoked. For the Spirit of the Lord says, it is now time for the enemy to pay up. It's time for you to deliver. It's time for your divine inheritance. It's time for you to push for your due season is here.   The Spirit of the Lord says, just as the wind is blowing so am I. There is a shaking. There is a shifting. There is a noise and there is a coming together. It's time for you to eat the wealth of nations. It's time for people to look at you and see God. You may have thought it was delayed or it was not going to happen. But the Lord said there is a divine appointment for I am the one who changes times and seasons.

God is getting ready to cause you to eat the wealth of nations. God is positioning you for delivery. It's time for you to deliver. It's time for you to break out of the holding pattern of that place that had you stagnated—that place that had you stuck. Your wilderness experience has come to an end. It's time for you to push. There is no longer any room in this dimension. You have to shift so that you can align yourself to take your proper place. It's time for you to deliver. For your due season has come. Your season has changed.

WELCOME TO THE NEXT CHAPTER

Our seasons have been designed to strip away those things that are not pleasing to the Lord. They are fixed in order to mold, shape, and develop us. The Bible declares that blows and wounds are purifiers. (Proverbs 20:30) Even when we find ourselves in hard places, they too have an assignment.

About the Author

Pastor Linda Scott is the senior Pastor of Kingdom Model Ministries located in Baltimore, Maryland. Linda is a successful entrepreneur. She is the owner of Trans4mations hair Salon & Boutique. She is the CEO and founder of No More Tears Movement, which is a 501c3 non-profit organization that focuses on healing and restoration for individuals who have been impacted by various forms of trauma. To connect with Pastor Linda Scott, visit:

- www.kingdommodelministries.com
- Instagram: Kingdom Model Ministries
- Facebook: Kingdom Model Ministries
- Email: Kingdommodelministries@gmail.com

www.ingramcontent.com/pod-product-compliance
Lightning Source LLC
Chambersburg PA
CBHW032137090426
42743CB00007B/621